Our Heroes

How Kids are Making a Difference

written and illustrated by Janet Wilson

Second Story Press

To my dear friend Barbara Marshall,
the kind heart and soul of Eden Mills

"If you think you're too small to make a difference, you haven't slept in a closed room with a mosquito."

(African Proverb)

The Ubuntu Story

A group of children played under the blazing African sun. They didn't have toys, but they were laughing, running, and jumping – as all children do. Nearby, an anthropologist watched, studying the customs and behavior of their Xhosa culture. Struck with an idea for an experiment, she said, "Let's have a contest." The children watched her place a basket of fruit under an umbrella thorn tree. "Whoever runs the fastest and reaches the basket first wins the fruit." Without hesitation, the children took each other's hands and ran together toward the tree. As they sat under the tree enjoying their sweet treats, the scientist asked, "Why did you run together when the fastest one could have had all the fruits for himself?"

"*Ubuntu!*" they shouted. "Ubuntu!"

The scientist was puzzled. "Is there an English word with the same meaning?"

No one could think of a word or phrase that meant 'ubuntu'.

"I am because we are," said a boy, and the others nodded.

"But what does that mean?" asked the scientist.

He said, "How can one of us be happy if all the other ones are sad?"

"The heart is like a garden. It will grow compassion or fear, resentment or love. What seeds will you plant there?" —Mahatma Gandhi

Ubuntu is a word that describes a way of living. It encourages us to treat each other with kindness because all humans are connected. Ubuntu is compassion for ourselves, for others near and far, and for the Earth. Ubuntu is *our humanity*.

The human species survives because we help one another. Babies need care, love, and nourishment if they are to thrive and reach adulthood. Perhaps this is why young people understand ubuntu – why they want all children to grow up in a safe and healthy environment. Some say this kind of wishful thinking is impossible, or even childish.

"The world needs childish thinking: bold ideas, wild creativity, and especially optimism," said Adora Svitak. She was twelve when she gave a lecture to adults about what they can learn from children. "Kids can be full of inspiring aspirations and hopeful thinking, like my wish that no child goes to bed hungry."

The children in this book never set out to be heroes or to be famous, but in acting on the kindness in their hearts, they have made a difference. They have all planted seeds of compassion and love.

—Janet Wilson

"We kids still dream about perfection. And that's a good thing because in order to make anything a reality, you have to dream about it first."
Adora Svitak, 12, USA

Adora was seven when she wrote her first book, *Flying Fingers*.

The traditional definition of a hero is a man of distinguished courage or ability, admired for his brave deeds and noble qualities. We define our young heroes as regular people of any age or gender, rich or poor, admired for their qualities of giving, sharing, helping, and caring.

"If the world had more ubuntu, we would not have war. We would not have this huge gap between the rich and the poor. You are rich so that you can make up what is lacking for others. You are powerful so that you can help the weak, just as a mother or father helps their children."
—Archbishop Desmond Tutu

"There is no point for others to have so much to eat while others have nothing to eat."

Andrew is hoping to be a pilot some day.

Andrew stared at the skeleton-thin Somali children on the TV news, their gaunt eyes gazing lifelessly from hollow sockets. He had seen hungry children in his own country, but he understood this was much worse – these babies and children were starving to death. Andrew's father explained that a long drought had caused a famine affecting more than twelve million people across East Africa. Tens of thousands of people had fled to refugee camps; almost thirty thousand children had died in just a few months. "This is not right," Andrew said. "Son, there's no need for you to worry about children so far away," his father replied. But Andrew, haunted by what he saw, decided to spend his school break trying to help the kids of Somalia who needed food the most. He bought T-shirts and stencilled "Save Somali Children From Hunger" on them, then walked from office to office in his city collecting donations – more than $6,000. He asked newspapers and television stations to raise awareness for his cause. He even tried to get on a reality show to raise money. When they refused, Andrew became more ambitious and raised his goal to $13 million. Andrew believes that a new era of hope for the future is beginning for African children, and children are playing an important part in building the Africa of their dreams.

Andrew says:
Think about our brothers and sisters who are suffering, not ourselves alone.

Hunger is the world's greatest solvable problem. The planet has an abundance of food, yet more than a billion people, mainly in underdeveloped countries, do not get enough to be healthy. Meanwhile, obesity is the number one health problem in some developed countries.

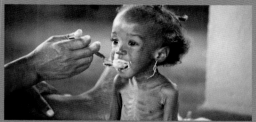

"Small actions can and will change the world around us for the better." **Adib Ayay**, 15, Morocco. When Adib thanked a local farmer for a gift of apples, he was shocked by the man's poverty. The farmer wasn't getting fair prices for his crops, so he encouraged the farmers to improve their businesses by using mobile technology. When earnings increased by more than 70%, Adib started Fair Farming, a student-run organization that promotes fair trade, empowers farmers, and fights hunger and poverty.

"Hunger is not a problem. It is an obscenity. How wonderful it is that nobody need wait a single moment before starting to improve the world." —Anne Frank

Hannah Taylor, 8, Canada

"No one should have to eat out of a dumpster."

National Red Scarf Day (Jan. 31) shows support and care for people who are hungry and homeless.

"When I was five, I saw a man eating out of a garbage can. I was very sad and felt sick about it. I asked my mom why he had to do that. She explained that the man didn't have a home. Later, I saw another homeless person. Everything she had was in one grocery cart. My heart was too sad. Everybody needs a home. I love my home. My mom told me that when you feel sad about things, if you do something to change the problem, your heart won't feel so sad. She was right. When I was eight, I started The Ladybug Foundation to help the homeless. Ladybugs are my mascot because they bring good luck, and homeless people need good luck. I painted cans and jars to look like ladybugs and used them to raise money. Since then, I have learned a lot about homelessness. One time, when I was leaving a shelter for homeless teenagers, I gave all the kids a hug. One quiet girl stepped forward and said, 'Until today I thought nobody liked me, but now I know that you like me.' I believe that if people knew there are others living without a home, they would want to help. I don't worry so much anymore because I know I can help and so can you."

Hannah says:

We all need to share a little of what we have and care about each other always.

Everyday, homeless people struggle to survive. Homeless youth suffer from injuries, diseases, and mental health problems. Many live in shelters or bunk with friends; some are fleeing abusive situations.

"You can't judge a book by its cover. These people are nice, kind – just like us. They just need a little extra help." **Sarah Lewis**, 7, Canada. When Sarah met Joe in a homeless shelter, she asked what he needed. Joe replied, "Socks." That inspired Sarah to start a campaign, Socks Warm Your Heart, that resulted in donations of several thousand pairs of socks.

"Volunteers not only give their time; they give their talents, creativity, and care back to the community. There's nothing stronger than the heart of a volunteer." **Bilaal Rajan**, 12, Canada. Bilaal launched the Barefoot Challenge. On International Children's Day, people go barefoot to remind others that millions of children have no shoes.

Kyle Weiss, 13, USA

"Every kid deserves the chance to play."

Kyle poses with the world's future soccer stars.

Kyle and his brother Garrett are crazy about soccer. When they aren't kicking around a ball, they're watching games on TV or attending matches. When they were 13 and 15 years old, their family attended a World Cup game in Germany where they felt the passion of the fans. At the game, Garrett and Kyle shared stories with some enthusiastic fans from Angola where soccer was a luxury most families couldn't afford. Kyle and Garrett realized how fortunate they were to have grown up with good fields, equipment, and organized teams with matching uniforms. They felt that African children deserved the same. At first they raised money to buy uniforms and soccer balls, but then they realized it was also important to build soccer fields. Their efforts were so successful that they started FUNDaFIELD and built several fields across Africa where children have experienced trauma or conflict. Kyle and Garrett learned the healing benefits of soccer for orphans, victims of diseases like HIV/AIDS, and children who'd been child soldiers. At fields built near schools, attendance and enrolment increased dramatically. Sport provides fun, improves mental and physical health, improves social skills, builds friendships, and teaches important life skills. At their soccer tournaments for kids, the prizes are goats!

Kyle says:

Find something you're passionate about. It will make it ten times better doing something you love and make it easier to do the hard stuff you don't like.

"Listen carefully and feel every story you hear from the other side. Imagine that you are the one who lives this story and then reflect." **Udda El-Hadalin**, 13, Palestine. Udda lives in a poor village with a prolonged history of tension and conflict with a neighboring Israeli settlement. Udda encourages youths to play soccer together and live peacefully with each other.

"Sport has the power to change the world. It has the power to inspire. It has the power to unite people in a way that little else does. It speaks to youth in a language they understand. Sport can create hope where once there was only despair. It is more powerful than governments in breaking down racial barriers."
—Nelson Mandela

"If God has made us all equal, why is there discrimination in God's temple itself and outside too?"

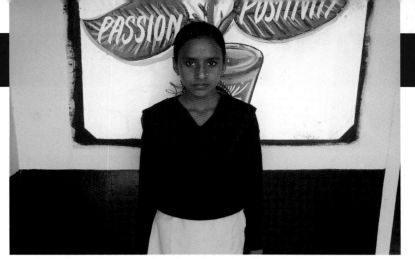

Arti was unhappy when her friend suffered discrimination.

It was an exciting day in Arti's village – the opening of a new temple. Arti arrived with her best friend, but Babita refused to enter. Much of India still believed in an ancient system of ranking people by "castes" and both girls knew that people born into a low caste were not permitted in temples. Arti thought this was unfair; she and Babita did everything together. Arti pulled her friend inside. Elderly villagers scolded and threatened them. One yelled, "If 'untouchables' are allowed, no one will come here for worship!" Many people left. Both girls cried in humiliation, but Arti hated this discrimination. She wanted change. She told a respected village leader, "In school we learn that the Indian constitution gives every citizen the same rights of freedom, life, and education. Prejudice based on religion and caste is illegal." With his support, Arti spoke to the village about her dream of a community free of discrimination. Her classmates staged rallies and skits and slowly, villagers started accepting untouchables. Lower caste children were allowed in schools; some adults found employment. As news spread, other villages also worked to abolish the caste system. The Buddha said, "A thousand candles can be lighted from the flame of one candle, and the life of the candle will not be shortened." Arti's spark lit such a candle.

Arti says:
If you have the will and the heart, even a small girl like me can become an agent for social change.

Millions of children live with discrimination, even though everyone is entitled to the same rights, regardless of race, sex, religion, disability, or other status. These children are vulnerable to violence and exploitation such as child labor. Many are denied access to schools and medical treatment.

"We taught people not to call the disabled people by nicknames." **Rasmita Engels**, 10, India. Her community believed Rasmita's difficulty in walking due to polio was caused by a curse from a previous life, so she wasn't allowed to go to school. Rasmita founded Good Friends Club to help other physically challenged children.

"Compassion can be put into practice if we realize that we are all members of humanity and the human family regardless of the difference in religion, race, color, or creed. Deep down there is no difference." —The Dalai Lama

Jonathan Lee, 13, South Korea/USA

"One person, one idea. That's all it takes to make a change."

Children marched to promote peace on the Korean peninsula.

A narrow strip of barren land – strewn with land mines and barbed wire – separates North and South Korea. Combat-ready troops have stood guard there since 1953, when a war between the two countries stopped. But Jonathan, born in South Korea and raised in the USA, had a vision for an area free from hostility, where children from both sides could play together in peace. He imagined children planting a forest of trees as a symbol of unity. Jonathan wrote to global leaders about his idea for the Children's Peace Forest. "This will plant the seeds for future peace and cooperation between the two nations," he wrote. "People may say that there's no hope and there's too much conflict for this to happen, but I see hope." Jonathan founded International Cooperation of Environmental Youth (ICEY) when he was 12, and the organization's motto is "Helping Our Polluted Earth" (HOPE). The two acronyms said together sound like 'I See Hope.' Jonathan's activism started early. When he was ten, he created GoGreen Man, an online environmental superhero, and delivered his go-green message to powerful people, including US President Obama. After meeting the South Korean president, Jonathan was granted the rare permission to enter North Korea, where he was well received by officials. His visit made worldwide headlines.

Jonathan says:

It is ICEY's hope that everyone can work together for humanitarian environmentalism – helping out people and the Earth.

"We wouldn't have been able to do it without the adults, but it was… the children who showed the way. We are tired of violence. We want to be able to go to the park or the forest without being afraid to step on a land mine. The adults must understand that we have the right to be children and the right not to be afraid to go out." **Mayerly Sanchez**, 15, Colombia. After her friend was stabbed to death, Mayerly helped found the Colombian Children's Movement for Peace, mobilizing two million children to create gun and violence-free zones in a country plagued by war and violence. Mayerly, far left, is shown with the other founders of the CCMP and Archbishop Desmond Tutu.

"It is easy enough to be friendly to one's friends. But to befriend the one who regards himself as your enemy is the quintessence of true religion." —Mahatma Gandhi

Alaina Podmorow, 9, Canada

"The only way you can make change in this world is to take action."

Alaina visited schoolgirls in Afghanistan in 2012.

"The worst thing you can do is nothing." Alaina heard these words from a Canadian journalist and human rights activist at a lecture about the treatment of girls and women in Afghanistan. "Sally Armstrong told so many stories about girls who were just like me and my friends," Alaina says. "But, instead of going to school and playing with friends, they were forced to stay home. They had no freedom and they were afraid they would be hurt or even killed. It just felt so wrong to me. That is why I decided to start raising money to educate Afghani girls. Even though it may only make a small difference, it still would make change." Alaina founded Little Women for Little Women in Afghanistan when she was nine. Her goal was to raise $750, enough for one teacher's annual salary. Since then, LW4LW has spread across Canada and the USA, raising money to train teachers, pay salaries, buy books, and support an orphanage, bringing equal education and opportunity to Afghani girls and women. "I believe that education equals peace. When you are educated, you become a stronger person. Illiteracy leaves people afraid of the unknown. When you are educated, you understand that people are all the same and deserve the same rights...." In 2012, Alaina spoke to the United Nations on the International Day of the Girl.

Alaina says:

Just as important as fundraising is raising awareness on the necessity for the global community to take action for the rights of women and girls.

"I dream of a world where girls no longer are victims of violence at the hands of men." **Mumtaz Bibi**, 15, Afghanistan. When she refused to marry a middle-aged man, the scorned man poured acid on Mumtaz's face and body. Although severely scarred, Mumtaz risks her life by speaking against violence.

International Day of the Girl, October 11, is meant to empower girls to reach their potential and decide their own future. In many countries, girls are more likely to live in poverty, especially in poor regions where they are the most disadvantaged people on the planet. Girls are often denied education, medical care, and food. An educated girl is more likely to raise the standard of living for herself, her family and her community.

"If you are not going to give the new generation pens, the terrorists will give them guns." —Malala Yousafzai, 15, Pakistan/UK

Kesz Valdez, 13, Philippines

"We can change the world one heart at a time.
And it starts with helping one person."

Kesz enjoys giving Gifts of Hope to underprivileged kids.

When his guardian asked seven-year-old Kesz, "What is your birthday wish?" he looked puzzled. Kesz didn't know about parties or presents or cakes, and he had no idea what it meant to make a wish. He had only recently learned about birthdays when his guardians had discovered his birth certificate. Once it was explained, Kesz knew exactly what he wanted – for all the poor children he knew to feel as happy as he did on that special day. Instead of gifts, Kesz asked for something that kids who worked in the local dump really needed – flip-flops. In his early years of misery, Kesz's own feet were cut climbing over piles of garbage to search for something to sell so his abusive father could buy drugs and alcohol. Kesz was only four when he ran away. Alone and frightened, he slept in a cold, graveyard tomb at night and scavenged each day. Once he was pushed into a pile of burning tires. That incident changed his life forever – Kesz was rescued and finally given love. "The fire that burned my skin is the same fire that started a flame in my soul." After his birthday, Kesz started Caring Children. "I did not have money but I had a lot of love to give." In addition to giving Gifts of Hope (clothes, toys, and shoes), Kesz taught children about basic sanitation so they could live healthier lives. In 2012, he was awarded the International Children's Peace Prize.

Kesz says:

One is never too young to do something to help and meet a need. The simple ways of sharing a meal, a toy, a pair of flip-flops, or a smile will bring joy.

UNICEF estimates that half of the world's children live in poverty. Being deprived of safe water, adequate shelter, food necessities, and health services prevents children from reaching their potential. Poverty robs them of their childhood.

"I enjoy my pathway to making a difference. You may also have your own pathway. You will not lose anything by giving, instead you will get many things that you never expect." **Muhamad Iman Usman**, 14, Indonesia. Iman has been inspiring young people to change the world and become future leaders since he opened a free library for kids when he was ten.

"Always put yourself in others' shoes. If you feel it hurts you, it probably hurts the other person too." —Unknown

"I want young people to know that it can be 'cool to care' –
for yourself, for others, and for the environment."

At 13, Luke was the youngest Chief Executive Officer in his country.

Elementary school was a struggle for Luke, but life became much worse in high school. Boys taunted him about being overweight and dyslexic, and verbal abuse escalated to pushing and shoving. "Bullying changed me from a happy, confident boy to someone who didn't want to speak. All I wanted to do was hide. I felt lonely, small; I lost all my confidence." One day, Luke was beaten so badly he was hospitalized. While recovering, he wanted to talk to other bullied kids to learn how to cope with his situation, but he was unable to find such help. That inspired him to found Young Pioneers. With his parents, he designed an anti-bullying program for schools. He trained volunteers, many who had been bullied themselves, providing them with the skills to lead change. Those young people taught others and became positive role models. Since then, Young Pioneers has helped thousands of kids. The organization gives scholarships to vulnerable children and teaches kids about the dangers of social network sites that make it easier for bullies to attack and stay hidden. "I'm not special. My inspiration comes from my drive to change the world and make a difference, to... show the bullies that I can overcome what they did to me," Luke says. "The project allowed me to step out, to walk with my head high."

Luke says:

Be responsible for your own actions and understand the impact that they can have on others. When we laugh, take part, or turn a blind eye, we are as bad as the bully.

Bullying is society's most common form of violence. Many people are verbally and physically abused because they are seen as different. Bullied children are more likely to struggle academically and face other challenges in life.

"You control your body but I don't control mine." **Jaylen Arnold**, 8, USA. Believing that kids teased him because they didn't understand his vocal outbursts and body tics, Jaylen began giving presentations to schools across the US to educate young people about Tourette syndrome, autism, and obsessive-compulsive disorder. Jaylen offers an anti-bullying curriculum and gives out *Bullying No Way* wristbands.

"Treat everyone with kindness, not because they are kind, but because you are." —Anonymous

Mimi Ausland, 12, USA

"Every dog and cat deserves a decent dinner."

Mimi and furry friend cuddle atop donations.

Mimi's parents had a nickname for their daughter – Dr. Doolittle. From the time she was two, Mimi rescued animals, including a bird injured by a dog, a worm stuck in the middle of a sidewalk, and a rainbow trout stranded in a canal. She also cared for a dog, a cat, a hamster, tropical fish, and two horses. She said, "I love all my pets more than the world!" Mimi started visiting the local humane society when she was seven and began volunteering as a pet socializer two years later. After learning that there were food shortages for thousands of dogs and cats in shelters across the country, Mimi wanted to help. With help from her parents, she created the websites Freekibble.com and Freekibblekat. com where she posted daily pet care questions. Each answer, whether right or wrong, added ten pieces of kibble to shelter donations. Local businesses and pet stores were first to donate cash and kibble. At the end of each month, Mimi delivered food to local humane societies. The sites are now two of the most visited animal rescue websites in the world. Animals in shelters and food banks have received millions of meals. Mimi then created Freekibble Cares to help even more animals, such as street dogs in Thailand, orphaned elephants in Zambia, and wild mustangs in the US.

Mimi says:

Your age doesn't matter. You can be six or sixty; just try to make something happen.

A child who extends kindness and mercy to animals is more considerate to others. Children who abuse animals are more likely to be abusive adults.

James meets his hero, Jane Goodall.

"When I began Ape-Aware, I had a speech impediment that made it difficult for people to understand me. It was hard, but I knew that gorillas couldn't speak for themselves and if I didn't, then who would?" **James Brooks**, 11, Canada. At age eight, when James learned that the great apes were threatened by poaching and deforestation, he began raising awareness and money to protect the species, their habitat, and help raise the standard of living of the people living in their regions.

"Let us develop respect for all living things. Let us try to replace violence and intolerance with understanding and compassion. And love."
—Jane Goodall

Taiyo Boily, 7, Canada/Japan

"I wanted to help the kids living in shelters."

Taiyo poses with his baseball idol, Roberto Alomar.

Taiyo was living in Japan when a massive earthquake and tsunami hit the island nation. "I thought I was gonna die for sure," Taiyo recalled. "I was under a table, crying. Things were flying off the shelves and the whole house was shaking." Fortunately the Boily family was unharmed, but thousands of people died and tens of thousands were left homeless. Taiyo wanted to do something to help, but his family left Japan soon after the natural disaster. Almost a year later, when his parents told him children were still living in shelters, Taiyo said, "I want to raise some money to help those kids." But what could a seven-year-old do? Taiyo loved baseball. It was his favorite thing in the world. He loved pitching, hitting, taking dives, and fielding. He practiced every day with his dad. So what better way to raise money than by hitting baseballs? Taiyo, a switch hitter, came up with a plan to raise $500 by charging fifteen cents for every right-handed hit he made and twenty cents for every left. On the first anniversary of the quake, Taiyo hit 162 fair balls right handed and 138 left handed. He donated more than $4,000 to Save the Children Canada to help with the Japan relief efforts. The next year, Taiyo held another marathon fundraising event for local kids who cannot afford to play sports.

Taiyo says:

If you want to do something and your parents say no, keep bugging them to let you do it.

"My name is Charlie Simpson. I am going to cycle around our local park as many times as possible (at least 7 miles I hope!). Please, can you sponsor me for UNICEF's Haiti Earthquake Children's appeal?" **Charlie**, 7, UK, sent this appeal over the Internet and raised more than £160,000 ($250,000 US) in 24 hours.

"To the world, you may just be one person, but to one person, you might be the world." **Grace Li**, 12, USA, and her siblings founded We Care Act, to help kids who survived a 2008 earthquake in China. Now they help other needy children recover from disasters, and engage youth around the world to help kids in need.

"If you want others to be happy, show compassion. If you want to be happy, show compassion." —The Dalai Lama

Kids Take Action!

"We thought we would all come to school dressed like Danny and show Danny that we love him very much." **Tommy Cooney**, 11, USA. Danny Keefe, 6, liked wearing a tie, suit, and fedora to school, even during his duties as the official water coach for his school's football team. When quarterback Tommy Cooney learned kids were teasing Danny because of his clothes and a speech problem, he rallied 40 teammates to dress like Danny for "Danny Appreciation Day."

"I used to hate lions, but now my invention is saving my father's cows and the lions." **Richard Turere**, 11, Kenya. Like other Maasai boys, Richard was responsible for the safety of his father's cows. But lions would come at night and kill their livestock. While patrolling his cowshed in the dark, Richard made a discovery – lions were afraid of his moving flashlight. This led to his invention – a simple and low-cost flickering light system to trick the lions into thinking that someone was around. It worked! Richard set up several other systems free of charge. Now his idea is being used all over Kenya for scaring away other predators like hyenas and leopards, saving many endangered animals from being killed by angry farmers.

"I know much how much pictures in the media have an effect on girls' body image. Girls want to be accepted, appreciated, and liked. When they don't fit the criteria, this can lead to eating disorders, dieting, depression, and low self-esteem." **Julia Bluhm**, 14, USA. After Julia collected 84,000 names on a petition asking *Seventeen* to stop altering photos and to show a diverse range of beauty, the teen magazine promised to never digitally change the size of a girl's face or body to make them appear slimmer or flawless.

"When one sees a situation that appears to be hopeless there is still hope. I believe that each person can change the world a little bit at a time." **Ana Dodson**, Peru/USA. When Ana was eleven, she visited her homeland of Peru. Shocked by the extreme poverty of orphans she met in a girl's home near her birthplace, Ana realized her good fortune to have been adopted. Ana founded Peruvian Hearts to empower girls in Peru through education and mentorship to become leaders within their communities. The organization provides a multivitamin and nutritious lunch to about 150 school children.

"Is our motive in life to blend in and find a space or to make a space and leave a positive legacy?" **Choc'late Allen**, 13, Trinidad & Tobago. Child actress and singer, Choc'late, was disturbed by the rising youth crime rate. Inspired by peace activist, Mahatma Gandhi, she conducted a public fast for five days, urging the nation to take personal responsibility for their thoughts, words, and actions. Following her fast, Choc'late toured schools, communities, and prisons across the Caribbean to spread her message: "We have the power of making the right choices! We have the power of accepting responsibility for our action! We have the power of doing anything!"

"The other children looked at me like I was a kind of monster. Everyone at school was scared and kept away from me. I was so ashamed I never left the house. If my only friend hadn't encouraged me to carry on, I would have never returned to school." **Thai Thi Nga**, 16, Vietnam. Nga was born with defects caused by the toxic chemical Agent Orange, which was used decades earlier in a brutal war. Nga courageously spoke out for compensation on behalf of other victims.

"If you have the ability to help people, then you have the responsibility to help." **Max Wallack**, 12, USA. After Max experienced life with his Great Gram who had dementia, he was inspired to launch Puzzles To Remember, a company that designs, collects, and donates puzzles that serve as a calming influence and therapeutic tool for Alzheimer's patients.

Kids Create!

"I would like to spread a good message with my brush." **Anjali Chandrashekar**, India, began drawing at the age of 4. When she was 6 years old, she began selling her work to raise funds and awareness for environmental, health, and humanitarian organizations. Anjali's painting was used as a poster for the UN Year of Bio-Diversity in 2010.

"To be an artivist, you need to know: What are your talents? What cause are you passionate about? How can you use your talent to raise money? No amount is too small, so start small." **Quinn**, **Jan**, and **Liam Dubé** began singing their mother's favorite songs to cheer her up during her battle with cancer. After her death, "Canada's Youngest Rock Band" began busking to fundraise for cancer research. Since then, the Brothers Dubé have performed at major music festivals, raising thousands of dollars for humanitarian causes from cancer charities to Haitian orphans.

"We must make the formation of character in children a priority, because they are the future of the nation. They have the power to change the world!" **Hector Ferronato**, 15, Brazil. As a child, Hector felt a deep love for Earth, but he despaired that other young people didn't also care about environmental problems such as deforestation and pollution. That inspired Hector and his friend Igor Rafael to create the website, O Mundo de Piata (Piata's World) with games that teach the next generation how to preserve, restore, and improve the environment and care for the planet.

"I want to help end childhood obesity, because I want everyone to be healthy, exercise, and stay in shape." **Chi Chi Monet**, 9, USA. Singer and rapper, Chi Chi, is inspiring kids to make good choices with her positive lyrics on issues like Bullying, Stranger Danger, and Eating Well.

"Never forget what it feels like to be treated differently and treat people the way you wish to be treated." **Jennifer Smith**, 12, USA. Even though Jenny has dyslexia, a neurological glitch that causes difficulty with reading, she wrote a book: *Dyslexia Wonders: Understanding the Daily Life of a Dyslexic from a Child's Point of View*. Proceeds go to help young people who struggle with the shame, anxiety, and loneliness associated with learning disabilities.

"I want to help people with autism participate more fully in the world around them." **Kayla Cornale**, 14, Canada. Inspired by her cousin's keen ability to memorize songs, Kayla devised a way to teach her how to talk, read, and express emotions through melodies played on a piano. *Sounds into Syllables – A Teaching System for Autistic Children* created a breakthrough in autism research.

"Being understood with empathy by others greatly relieves our distressed hearts." **Naoki Higashida**, 13, Japan. Unable to speak, Naoki used a Japanese language alphabet board to write, *The Reason I Jump: The Inner Voice of a Thirteen-Year-Old Boy with Autism*. His book provides greater understanding of the hearts and minds of children with autism.

"Even something as ugly as a bullet fired in a war can be made beautiful if you are willing to work to change it into something else." **Lovetta Conto**, 14, Liberia. For ten years, Lovetta lived in a war refugee camp where she tried to stay strong. "I envisioned myself as a tree growing up, growing fruit and giving my fruit to other people who needed help." She created the *Akawelle* (love) necklace from bullets and metal casings. The "LIFE" inscription shows that even after war, new life can begin. Proceeds go to a home and school in Liberia for young people affected by war and poverty.

What YOUth Can Do

Make the World Better!

"I want the world to be a better place." **Toby Little**, 5, UK. After reading a book about how a mailed letter reaches another country, Toby asked, "Mummy, can I write a letter to the world?" And that's what he did – Toby hand-wrote over 400 letters to 200 different countries. When he learned that some people couldn't afford a stamp to mail a return letter, Toby decided to do something to help the poor. He asked for donations to ShelterBox, a charity that helps families who have lost everything in a disaster.

Help Others

"I know what it is like to be scared and alone and I don't want other kids to go through that." **Jessica Carscadden**, 11, China/USA. Adopted from an orphanage in China at five years old, Jessica knew that simple comforts, like having a stuffed animal to hold, help children in frightful situations. She brought her own teddy bears to the local fire station so that first responders could hand them out to young victims of trauma. When she saw how they calmed the children, Jessica started the We Care Bear Project to reach even more children.

Donate

"Young leaders who make a difference give other youths someone to look up to." **Jaevin Spero**, 11, Canada. Jaevin and Dakota Lamb thought all kids should feel special on their birthday. When the two learned that some parents can't afford luxuries like presents, cakes, or balloons, they founded Wonderful Wishes to grant birthday wishes for children in need. At first they donated their own money, but then they asked local businesses to help. They've since granted over 150 birthday wishes. Dakota said, "Before we started this I didn't even know how many people needed help."

Volunteer

"Kindness is the only thing that you need." **Otra Phillips**, 5, USA. Giving hugs, serving dessert, reciting poems, and reading stories are just a few of the many kind things Otra does for seniors at her local care center. Otra says volunteering makes her feel happy, "Because it shows them that you care."

Fundraise

"I am a bit like a penny. By myself, I am not worth much. But with a little help and lots of pennies, you can achieve a lot." **Jeneece Edroff**, 7, Canada. After living with a painful condition that required several surgeries, Jeneece understood the challenges faced by those who need medical care and their caregivers. She began collecting pennies to give back to the children's charity that had helped her. Jeneece raised over five million dollars to build a "home away from home" for families who have to travel for medical treatments.

Create or Join an Organization

"It's not about doing someone else a favor. When we open our arms and our hearts to people with disabilities, we all benefit...and learn from each other's unique gifts and talents. I have learned more than I ever could have imagined working with the Sparkles, and I've also made some of the best friends I've ever had." **Sarah Cronk**, 15, USA. Sarah watched her older brother with autism struggle to make friends until a popular captain invited him to join the swim team. When her brother's confidence soared from this simple act of kindness, Sarah decided to create a cheer team for students with and without disabilities. The Sparkle Effect motto: "When everyone cheers, everyone wins."

Tell the World

"Kids are told not to be friends with transgender kids, which makes us very lonely and sad.... We like to make friends and want to go to school." **Sadie Croft**, 11, USA. Sadie, who socially transitioned from male to female in kindergarten, wrote a letter to President Barack Obama to ask why he mentioned gay people in a speech to his nation, but not trans people. Sadie's letter went viral over the Internet.

Acknowledgments

I extend my deeply felt thanks to the heroes who shared their remarkable stories in this book. I appreciate all the help they and their families provided, as well as the people I contacted in their organizations and foundations. I am grateful for the generous donations of images. Thanks to Juliet Zimmerman and Alexander Barnstijn for modeling. The Canada Council for the Arts and the Ontario Arts Council Writers' Reserve provided financial support so that I could complete this book. Thanks to the wonderful team of women at Second Story Press: Carolyn Jackson, Melissa Kaita, Emma Rodgers, Phuong Truong, Kathryn Cole, and Kelly Jones, with Margie Wolfe at the helm. My kind and devoted husband, Chris Wilson, was invaluable at all stages of this project, keeping me watered, fed, and managed, so that I was free and able to create.

For more information:

Adora Svitak: www.adorasvitak.com

Andrew Adansi-Bonnah: www.facebook.com/UNICEFGhana/posts/442480492465100

Adib Ayay: threedotdash.org/the-summit/global-teen-leaders/2013-global-teen-leaders/475-adib-ayay

Hannah Taylor: www.ladybugfoundation.ca

Sarah Lewis: sljhwin.wix.com/sockswarmyourheart

Bilaal Rijan: www.bilaalrajan.com

Jonathan Lee: www.iceyhope.org

Arti Verma: www.spiritofcommunityindia.com/winners_2013/Arti_Verma.html

Rasmita Engels: www.aaina.org.in

Luke Lancaster: lukelancaster.wordpress.com/author/lukelancaster

Jaylen Arnold: www.jaylenschallenge.org

Alaina Podmorow: www.littlewomenforlittlewomen.com

Kyle Weiss: www.fundafield.org

Mimi Ausland: www.freekibble.com/about.asp

James Brooks: great-apes.com

Kesz Valdez: c3champs.org.ph

Muhamad Iman Usman: www.imanusman.com

Grace Li: www.wecareact.org

Tommy Cooney and Danny Keefe: fundly.com/danimal-s-army-the-danny-keefe-fund

Julia Bluhm: www.change.org/petitions/seventeen-magazine-give-girls-images-of-real-girls

Ana Dodson: www.peruvianhearts.org

Choc'late Allen: www.facebook.com/pages/CHOCLATE-ALLEN/28653387117

Thai Thi Nga: Quotation is from the Globe Magazine. worldschildrensprize.org

Max Wallack: www.puzzlestoremember.org

Brothers Dubé: www.brothersdube.com

Chi Chi Monet: chichimonet.com

Hector Ferronato: www.omundodepiata.com.br/english/play

Lovetta Conto: www.akawelle.com

Jennifer Smith: jennyspeaks.com

Kayla Cornale: basef.ca/KaylaCornale

Anjali Chandrashekar: anjalichandrashekar.wordpress.com

Toby Little: www.writingtotheworld.com and www.justgiving.com/writingtotheworld

Jaevin Spero and Dakota Lamb: www.facebook.com/jaevinswonderfulwishes

Jessica Carscadden: www.wecarebears.com

Jeneece Edroff: www.rwglobal.com/~jeneece/index.html

Sarah Cronk: www.thesparkleeffect.org

Credits

art: courtesy of Juliet Zimmerman, 10, Canada

Adora: courtesy of Svitak family

Andrew: courtesy of Samuel Adansi-Bonnah

Hannah: ©Winnipeg Free Press, Trevor Hagan, November 13, 2009 reprinted with permission

Sarah: ©Nick Brancaccio/The Windsor Star

Jonathan: courtesy of Melissa Lee

CCMP: courtesy of Lydia Smith

Arti: courtesy of the Bharti Foundation

Rasmita: courtesy of International Children's Peace Prize

Luke: courtesy of Kathleen Lancaster

Jaylen: courtesy of Robin Arnold

Alaina and Mumtaz: courtesy of Alaina Podmorow

Kyle: courtesy of the Weiss family

Soccer: courtesy of Mifalot, Neighbors United program supported by the EU Partnership for Peace

Mimi: courtesy of J.Nichole Smith, dane-dane.com

James: courtesy of the Jane Goodall Institute of Canada

Kesz: courtesy of Kesz

Taiyo: courtesy of Milo Boily

Charlie: ©PA Photos Limited, UK

Tommy and Danny: courtesy of Jeannette Chiocca

Richard: ©Wildlife Direct, Dr. Paula Kahumbu

Ana: courtesy of Danny Dodson

Thai Thi Nga: courtesy of the World's Children's Prize

Quinn, Jan, and Liam: courtesy of the Brothers Dubé

Chi Chi Monet: ©Phelan Marc

cartoon: courtesy of Hector Ferronato

Akawelle necklace: courtesy of Lovetta Conto

art: courtesy of Anjali Chandrashekar

Toby: courtesy of Sabine Little

Jessica: courtesy of the Carscadden family

Otra: copyright George Sakkestad

Sarah: courtesy of The Sparkle Effect

Library and Archives Canada Cataloguing in Publication

Wilson, Janet, 1952-, author, illustrator
Our heroes : how kids are making a difference /
written and illustrated by Janet Wilson.

ISBN 978-1-927583-41-8 (bound)

1. Reformers—Biography—Juvenile literature. 2. Children—
Biography—Juvenile literature. 3. Social action—Juvenile literature.
I. Title.

HN19.W54 2014   j303.48'40922   C2014-902962-4

Text and illustrations copyright © 2014 by Janet Wilson
Design by Melissa Kaita

Second Story Press gratefully acknowledges the support of the Ontario Arts Council and the Canada Council for the Arts for our publishing program. We acknowledge the financial support of the Government of Canada through the Canada Book Fund.

Printed and bound in China

Canada Council   Conseil des Arts
for the Arts   du Canada

Published by
Second Story Press
20 Maud Street, Suite 401
Toronto, Ontario, Canada
M5V 2M5
www.secondstorypress.ca

FSC
www.fsc.org
MIX
Paper from
responsible sources
FSC® C019368